REVERSE MORTGAGES

by Jim Anderson

Amazon Books FIRST EDITION
ISBN# 978-1-893257-51-1

Every effort has been made to make this book as complete and accurate as possible. However, there may be mistakes in typography or content. Also, this book contains information on Reverse Mortgages only up to the publishing date. Therefore this document should be used as a guide only – not as a definitive source of Reverse Mortgage information.

INDEX

REVERSE MORTGAGE DANGERS

THE PROS, CONS, DRAWBACKS, DOWNSIDE & DISADVANTAGES

(I'm NOT From The Government, and I Really AM Here to Help You!)

FORWARD

Reverse Mortgage ads can be seen day and night on TV. One or another popular and "believable" personality, such as Fred Thompson and Robert Wagner, is paid to extoll the virtues of this poorly-understood and overly-hyped financial vehicle.

Simply call the phone number on your TV screen, receive a CD in the mail, be contacted by a "Reverse Mortgage Expert", and decide for yourself whether a Reverse Mortgage is right for you. Nothing to it, right? Wrong.

"Sales-terms", used liberally throughout the ads, such as: "safe", "effective", "government-insured", "tax-free cash", and "…an easy first step toward enjoying life more fully", can all be very appealing.

They can also be very misleading. I have literature from dozens of Reverse Mortgage providers, and there is not one negative consequence mentioned in any of them. Why would there be? This is SALES literature.

Heretic though I may be, consider this book to be my "anti-sales" literature!

1.THE ADVERTISED ADVANTAGES

Let's begin by listing the "Advantages" given as the reasons why a Reverse Mortgage is your perfect answer to entering nirvana. I copied this from an item of sales literature that was given to me for my own field use:

- You get money to pay off your debts and never make payments;

- The Reverse Mortgage is in effect as long as you live in the home or keep the loan;

- No payments ever need to be made with minimal homeowner obligation;

- You are guaranteed security;

- If you adhere to minimal requirements, the lender or government can never take your home;

- Title remains the same – lender receives only a mortgage lien;

- The extra cash you receive may help you to maintain your independence and security;

- You retain full control of everything;

- You can decide how much equity you will eventually use and how much you will leave to your heirs;

- You control how much cash you take out of your home's equity;

- Leave as much of your equity in place as you decide;

- Because of the age-graduated and conservative lending limits you are prevented from using up all of your home equity;

- The loan is safe and fair;

- The Reverse Mortgage is designed by the government, tightly regulated, and is an extensively disclosed program;

- Before you sign anything you need independent counseling for your protection;

- It is a fair and reasonable business transaction. Your lender is repaid only what it is owed.

On the surface this all looks like a pretty darn good deal. And once you know all of the possible drawbacks and pitfalls, you may even still believe that it is. But for most, it really is **not** what it might seem. Read on, and decide for yourself.

2. THE BANK

The "Occupy Wall Street" movement is an odd curiosity. One can view it as a group of paid anarchists and socialists who are part of an evil plot to "fundamentally change America". To a large extent their anger has been focused on "banks" in general, but for the most part they really have no idea what they want to see happen.

Wall Street "investment banks" are quite different from your local checking and savings banks, but they seem quite willing to vilify and vandalize the latter as well.

One could also view the Occupy Movement as a necessary call for restrictions on abuses, imagined or real. The fact is, love them or hate them, were it not for both investment banks **and** your local banks the United States would never have become the powerful world leader it has been for decades. We simply cannot exist without them.

<u>Both are in business to make money.</u> That's Capitalism, right or wrong, like it or not. They are not established to be non-profit.

Never lose sight of the fact that Reverse Mortgages are a **money-making business** for the banks. Banks are set up to earn as much of your money as possible. They will **always** hit you with the highest interest and charges they can get away with. This is why you should always shop around.

Never believe what you will be told that "banks are all the same". "Rates are all the same". These are not benevolent societies, nor should they be. They are money-making businesses. That is Capitalism. Period.

What I find egregious is the common practice of banks, the local lending-institution type, paying bonuses to their salespeople (read "Loan Originators") to charge you as much in fees and interest above some minimum bottom-line figure as they can. You simply need to be aware of that practice. I do know it exists, though I have never seen a study of how wide spread it may be.

One only has to look at the reports of irregularities at the defunct Countrywide Mortgage Company to understand what is possible. It has always been a "dirty" industry.

3. THE LOAN ORIGINATOR

The individual at the bank, or at the independent mortgage company, who takes your Reverse Mortgage Loan Application, is called a "Loan Originator". Until rather recently these individuals did not even have to hold any sort of license in most States!

Mortgage Loan Originators are also in business to make money....your money, just as is the bank. No altruism, just plain old Yankee capitalism. Most certainly there is nothing inherently wrong in this, business is business. But don't hold the impression that anyone in connection with a Reverse Mortgage transaction is doing you a favor out of the goodness of their hearts! Least of all the Loan Originator.

It is a seldom-reported fact, as I pointed out above, that many banks pay their Loan Originators a bonus for charging you the highest rate with which they can get away! They are bounty hunters and you are the bounty!

If you are intent on getting a Reverse Mortgage, please be certain to shop around.

You may be shocked at the different quotes you are likely to receive.

Remember, over time, even one-eighth of a percent difference between two mortgages can amount to a large sum of money.

4. QUALIFYING

Not everyone can qualify for a Reverse Mortgage, even if they **are** 62 years of age or older. The ads do not go out of their way to point out this fact. There are two possible reasons for this, an existing mortgage, and one's net income.

If you have a mortgage on your home, it is important to note that it is very possible that you cannot even qualify for a Reverse Mortgage because of it. There are many situations where you might very well have qualified for a Reverse Mortgage a number of years ago, but you cannot qualify today. This is due to the massive drop in property values and low appraisals relative to your outstanding mortgage balance.

If you owe more than your home is worth, the very common "under water" scenario, forget about even considering a Reverse Mortgage. In fact, based upon the percentage of the appraised value that you can get in a Reverse Mortgage, which is scaled based on your age, you will need to be considerably "above water" on your mortgage to even break even.

Say you have a home that was worth $300,000 a few years ago, but would only be appraised today at $200,000 (possibly a lot less). Your present "forward" mortgage is only $150,000, so you are well above water. No sweat, right?

But at age 62 you could only get around $100,000 today from a Reverse Mortgage, which doesn't begin to cover your present mortgage, let alone give you additional cash, even though you are "above water". Even in your 70s, where you get a higher amount of reverse mortgage money as a percentage of appraised value, you might still just barely cover the mortgage.

The other way you might not qualify is if you cannot show the financial ability to pay your real estate taxes and home repairs. His ability must be for the rest of your life in the home. The government has begun to see Reverse Mortgage foreclosures happen because of borrowers' inability to cover the required continuing expenses.

Uncle Sam has finally awakened to the need to assure that the catastrophic scenario created a few years back ith forward mortgages will not re-occur in the reverse arena. By forcing banks to make forward mortgage loans to individuals who could not possibly carry them after they adjusted upwards the government itself caused this entire housing price collapse mess. Don't blame the banks.

The government does not want to see this repeated with Reverse Mortgages in the future. Unfortunately, Reverse Mortgage foreclosures have actually begun to be a reality.

5. COUNSELING

If you are convinced by the marketing material and ads that you simply cannot live without a Reverse Mortgage, the government has set up a mandatory question and answer session with a government-licensed counselor. This must be with you and your spouse, and can be in person or on the telephone. In theory this is a really good idea. It is designed to take everyone who came before off the hook for possibly misrepresenting the product either from ignorance or by design.

You can ask the interviewer any questions you might have. By the end of the session you are supposed to have all of the information you need to make an educated decision. Once you complete the Q & A you will receive a lovely certificate in the mail, suitable for framing, attesting to the "fact" that you are ready to proceed. You in fact are not.

Incidentally, just to be certain you are serious and to weed out the curious, you must pay for the counselor interview up front . This is usually $75.00 to $125.00. Neither the Loan Originator (read "salesperson") nor whichever middleman-company or bank he or she represents can front you this money. Nor can it be "rolled into" the loan. Government rule.

You must pay it yourself up front. And no one can direct you to any one particular counselor/interviewer. You must select on your own from a very long list of counselors located nationwide. This is also good.

Call enough of them and you will almost always find one that is operating under a government grant and charges you absolutely nothing for the counseling! Some will even travel to your home for the interview. These government grants may not last forever, but a few do exist at this writing. As far as I have been told few Loan Originators ever mention this potential freebie to a client. Most are not even aware of it.

Now up to here all of this sounds great: Lots of written information from a variety of sources, and a session with a trained counselor. I am certain the government intends for the system to fully protect the consumer. In reality it does not.

There are a number of flaws inherent in the counseling system. For starters, as with IRS personnel, you can ask three different counselors the same question and get three very different answers. Believe me, I have tested this on many occasions. You can do this yourself. There is a VAST difference between counselors. Some seem quite knowledgeable. Others seem quite clueless.

The problem is, you do not know all of the right questions to ask, and even if you did, the answers you receive might or might not be helpful.

6. WHY LISTEN TO ME?

Allow me to digress for a moment: "Who am I and why should you listen to or believe me?" Well, for starters, I have been licensed as a Loan Originator or Loan Officer for over twelve years, licensed in real estate for over forty years, and as a Financial Broker and Securities Principal for almost as long. I am a Registered Financial Planner.

Real Estate, Mortgages, and Finance have been "my thing" for my entire working career, either as an independent contractor, or as a high-level executive of a number of Fortune 500 Divisions.

I presently own my own Real Estate Brokerage, Insurance Brokerage, and Loan Origination companies. For the past six years I have focused 100% on doing my best to explain the many subtle nuances of Reverse Mortgages to individuals from 60 to 95 years of age.

I have spoken to groups, and to countless couples. I am a 75 year old financially-comfortable "retiree" and can assure you don't need the Reverse Mortgage commissions.

(And believe me, the commissions can be MASSIVE.) I am fully qualified to write this book.

Needless to say I am considered a heretic in the minds of many Reverse Mortgage Originators and Bankers. I believe unequivocally that at least nine out of ten individuals who have signed up for Reverse Mortgages were never fully aware of the many possible negative implications of doing so.

Many still are not, and many will live to regret their decision.

7. SO WHAT'S THE CATCH?

There are many ignored factors that almost NEVER come up during the application process. The salesperson (the "Loan Originator") is there to close the sale, not to put doubts in your mind. He or she can smell those commission and/or bonus dollars! Errors of omission, a tendency to ignore some rather serious negatives, abound.

Are there some cases where a Reverse Mortgage may make sense for you? Yes indeed, but they are few and far between and in my mind are "special" situations. I'll talk about them later.

So what are the negatives that are seldom if ever discussed? The following pages should give anyone considering a Reverse Mortgage at least some cause to pause. I offer these drawbacks in no particular order. Any one could be very important to you, and any one could be a "deal killer".

Many people hear about Reverse Mortgages and get all excited about the "free" money they are told they can get. Many of these become very disappointed when they learn that they cannot qualify even if they **are** older than 62, as I mentioned above.

Beyond that, the fact is that in a Reverse Mortgage you receive only a percentage of the **appraised** value of your home, and this percentage varies by your age at nearest birthday.

The older you are, the higher percentage of equity you can get. A super-senior might get 80% of the appraised value, a 62 year old perhaps 50%. These percentages are firmly set by the government, and they change from time to time.

The trend has been for them to go lower over time. No one can predict what limits the government may set in the future, nor guarantee that the program will even continue.

8.YOUR ENEMY THE APPRAISER

The problem that arises is that in today's depressed real estate market your home may be worth **far** less than you imagine. An appraiser must take into account recent comparable sales in your area. Many of these may be distressed "short-sales" or foreclosures, which greatly depresses your home value.

With so many bank-owned foreclosed-properties being sold for pennies on the dollar many seniors are shocked to learn just how little their house is actually worth these days. It is easy to remember the good old days, and to think of your home's value as the maximum it was ever worth historically.

Appraisers are sent out to your home by the lenders themselves (you have **no choice** of appraiser). They are VERY conservative in their evaluations. That's the way the banks want it, and the appraisers prefer to keep their jobs! They're not evil, just practical.

Much of the past housing bubble burst has been blamed on very liberal and unrealistically-high appraisals drawn up by appraisers who were often selected, from an "approved" list, by real estate salespersons and home owners to whom they had more allegiance than to the banks. Not any more. The banks are now in full control.

Very often you will not be told early on by the Loan Originator that you must pay **up front** anywhere from $350.00 to $550.00 for the privilege of finding out how little your home is actually worth in today's market!

Asking a local real estate professional for their opinion of your home's value is almost without purpose. They are not appraisers. They wear rose colored glasses. They do not want to insult or alienate you, so they invariably high-ball an "off the cuff" estimate request.

In any event, especially if you are trying to pay off an existing mortgage, you might be very disappointed to learn that you cannot qualify for all the cash that you need, if any. In fact, in the case of very low priced homes, you may not qualify **at all** if the ratio of the cost to you of obtaining the Reverse Mortgage is too high as a percentage of the money you could net. This is a seldom mentioned part of the law.

9.YOUR FUTURE IN YOUR HOME

Let's change the subject. Ask yourself this question: "Am I and my spouse going to live in this very same house for the rest of our lives with 100% certainty?" If the answer is anything other than an unqualified "Yes!", think twice about a Reverse Mortgage.

Statistically most couples move every five to seven years. In five or ten years the cost to get out of the Reverse Mortgage might be prohibitive. That interest against equity adds up quickly. And of course your upfront fees and commissions are lost forever. As we will discuss later, you might be forced to live there forever whether you care to do so or not.

Don't lose site of the fact that every month you will owe more money than you received. Over time this can be a lot more than you might imagine. It would be unlikely that you would have the cash required to buy out of the Reverse Mortgage at some later date. It is equally unlikely that you could qualify for a forward mortgage to cover the reverse one.

Ask for, and study closely, the amortization table based on the proposed Reverse

Mortgage loan. It is buried in the immense package of Reverse Mortgage documentation. You need to study this carefully before you take even the most preliminary steps. Sign nothing until you do. Any Loan Originator should be willing to provide this document up front.

Focus on the assumptions made, especially as regards the appreciation of the home over time. Anyone who tells you they know this present real estate market is about to dramatically turn around soon is either a liar or a fool.

Seek the advice of a qualified, independent professional, accountant, lawyer or financial planner, if you do not fully understand this appreciation vs interest-charged-against-equity document. Try plugging in some much lower appreciation estimates (these days close to zero) and you will be in for an unplewasant surprise!

10.   THE LOAN ORIGINATOR REVISITED

Also be aware that the Loan Originator (again, read "salesperson") with whom you are dealing may actually know very little about Reverse Mortgages! This is especially true if this person does not **specialize** only in Reverse Mortgages, as few do. Consider asking how many Reverse Mortgages he or she actually closed in the past month. Expect: "None".

You may be told (and the salesperson might actually believe) that the rates and fees are fixed by the government so it doesn't matter at all from whom you get your Reverse Mortgage. Nothing could be further from the truth.

Historically the lending industry has been the least regulated of all in the financial area. In many places there was no license required at all to originate loans. The licenses that did exist were extremely easy to obtain.

They still are easy to obtain, even though they are mandatory now. Many, if not most, Loan Originators are not the sharpest pencils in the box. They need not be to obtain a license. It is sort of like obtaining a real estate license, only easier. In general it does not attract rocket scientists! There are many excellent experienced Loan Officers and Realtors out there, but they are the exception, not the rule.

To this day there is NO specific "Reverse Mortgage License" for Loan Originators. If anyone tells you he or she is "licensed in Reverse Mortgages" they are telling you, at best, a very misleading half-truth. All Loan Originators are allowed to sell Reverse Mortgages. Very few do any at all. Some do a few.

Individuals specializing in Reverse Mortgages to the exclusion of forward mortgages are very few and far between.

I know of no bank whose local on-site "loan officer" only does Reverse Mortgages. I have "interviewed" (as a fake prospective client, naughty me) many bank-based Loan Originators who have been eager to do one for me but have demonstrated virtually no knowledge of the many nuances.

Often when I have asked: "What are the disadvantages to my taking out this Reverse

Mortgage?", I am told "There aren't any!".
Really?

There is an immense difference in the skill-set
required for selling plain old forward
mortgages as opposed to Reverse Mortgages.
Most Loan Originators become relatively
competent over time simply by processing so
many forward mortgage loan applications.
The do so few Reverse Mortgages that their
in-depth knowledge can be quite lacking.

Some Reverse Mortgage Originators are
members of "NRMLA", the National Reverse
Mortgage Lenders Association. Membership
is **not** mandatory for Reverse Mortgage
Originators.

The fact of membership certainly does NOT
insure that your Loan Originator knows any
more about Reverse Mortgages than a non-
NRMLA member. In fact, there are many non-
members who specialize 100% in Reverse
Mortgages who might well be a far better
source of advice.

NARMLA members are not required to take
any additional education. It is analogous to
real estate salespersons who may or may not

be "Realtors" (i.e., members of The National association of Realtors".) Same exact license, same exact licensing education.

In theory only, members of such "trade organizations (which are essentially lobbyists) are pledged to a maintain a code of ethics. I know of many very fine non-Realtor highly-ethical real estate salespersons, as well as equally fine Reverse Mortgage loan Originators who choose not to join NARMLA.

Although your Loan Originator may tell you otherwise, the mortgage loan interest percentage itself can vary between lenders. Even more so, the various fees can be very different. The government puts a cap on certain of these fees, but no **minimum**. Point is, you do have room to negotiate rates and fees.

If you are considering a Reverse Mortgage, shop around. There are many different direct bank lenders, and far more middleman mortgage brokers. All of these are out to make as much of your money as possible. Some are simply more greedy than others.

Buyer beware!

18.   THE LOAN APPLICATION

The basic paperwork with which a Loan Originator will begin the Reverse Mortgage loan process is identical to that used for a forward mortgage. The paperwork that follows later, however, is longer and far more complex and much harder to understand.

If you ever do ever apply for a Reverse Mortgage don't even THINK about fudging any initial application information, such as age, and income in particular.

The loan processors, those behind-the scenes folk employed by the lenders to scrutinize every paperwork detail, will definitely find your misstatements. The lender will disqualify you immediately.

In the past application "Funny-stuff", created what is known in the trade as "liar loans". In many cases the Loan Originators themselves would "fill in the blanks" to create an application that would guarantee qualification under specified debt to income ratios.

Such practices were once were very commonplace. These were the "no income verification" forward mortgage loans heavily promoted pre-bubble-burst. This sort of thing just no longer passes muster, period.

Of course, qualifying someone for a loan they could not afford, especially after their adjustable loans re-adjusted much higher, was not doing the borrower any sort of favor. These practices, albeit the result of the government mandating lender practices, led directly to the real estate crisis we face today.

12. THE PSYCHOLOGY OF MORTGAGES

A major negative to you becoming involved in a Reverse Mortgage is purely psychological.

Many senior folks have spent their entire lives struggling mightily to pay off various thirty-year mortgages and "second mortgage" home equity loans. Some finally breathed a giant sigh of relief that at long last they had accomplished that life-long dream....**no more mortgage!** "We finally own our house free and clear!". Party time! At least until now.

Here is where Reverse Mortgage "buyer's remorse" can set in. That nice comfortable feeling of "no mortgage burden" will soon be gone, probably forever. It is a factor well worth considering.

Psychologically, a mortgage is a mortgage, irrespective of whether monthly payments come out of your pocket or out of your home equity. You return to the "We don't really actually own our home" mentality. And you, in fact, do not.

Many purveyors of Reverse Mortgages will tell you: "It's not actually a "real" mortgage, it's just a "home equity conversion loan". It's a HECM, pronounced "heck em". Well heck, if it quacks like a duck and walks like a duck it ain't a llama! These are mortgages, period, semantics aside.

Don't be heckemed out of reality!

13.   TAX IMPLICATIONS

In a more tangible vein, many people enjoy one of the government's very generous tax benefits.   Homeowners can deduct the interest on the mortgage on their home when they file their taxes.

This benefit may not last forever, but it is in effect as I write this, as it has been for as long as I can remember. To a large extent this very generous deduction is why many individuals pay little or no income tax at all.

In fact, it weighs heavily on the very decision **TO** buy a house at all in the first place. It is the number one argument for buying rather than renting a home.

Take note: <u>REVERSE MORTGAGE INTEREST IS NOT TAX DEDUCTABLE</u> yearly during the life of the mortgage The moment you pay off your existing mortgage debt with a Reverse Mortgage's proceeds you give up this valuable yearly tax benefit.

This fact may be of little or no consequence to some. It is surely meaningless for those who have finally paid off their mortgage balances after years of hard work and have no tax deduction.

I have advised many a client to seek the advice of a tax professional to explain to them the impact on their finances that the loss of this valuable tax benefit would cause. Most have been relying upon it for years to legally minimize their tax burden. The true consequences of losing this benefit can be a shock!

Did you know you can actually <u>purchase</u> a home using a Reverse Mortgage? Most real estate salespersons haven't a clue how to do this, but it is possible and done fairly often by the real pros.

The problem here is the same as in the above case of losing your present mortgage-interest tax-deduction. What makes a house affordable to many is the positive impact on their net income taxes of the mortgage interest deduction. If you are considering buying a home with a Reverse Mortgage be sure to consider the tax implications.

Incidentally, you cannot have a Reverse Mortgage on a second home. Reverse

Mortgages only apply to your primary residence. Nor can you and your wife have two separate Reverse Mortgages on two separate properties, unless you live entirely apart and can prove it if necessary,

14. YOUR HEIRS – VULTURES OR SUPPORTERS?

Now here is another important consideration that many have pooh-poohed when I bring it up during my early discussions with clients: "What will your children and grandchildren think about you getting a Reverse Mortgage?". The response is almost always: "Why of course they'd want us to do this." **Think again.**

Reality: In my experience 50% of all adult children are **adamantly** against their parents getting a Reverse Mortgage, and the other half are just plain against it for a variety of reasons, or at best neutral! Perhaps one in twenty thinks that it is a really great idea for their parents to proceed with the transaction. Sadly, this reservation is for a very wrong reason.

It literally brings tears to my eyes (and quite often to the eyes of my clients) when I sit around a table with a senior couple who think that a Reverse Mortgage makes sense, and watch three to five siblings fume over the potentially-reduced proceeds of the estate once their parents are dead!

Apparently it never occurs to most senior couples that their kids are greedy little turds who just can't wait for mommy and daddy to croak so they can sell off the house and split the spoils. I've seen it time and time and time and time again. It is the rule, not the exception. Very sad.

You see, month by month, inexorably, the interest on the Reverse Mortgage is added to the amount "owed" to pay off the mortgage. Can the equity in the house keep pace with this interest burden? Certainly not in today's market, and probably not even close to it in the foreseeable future. Goodbye inheritance!

The fact is, every month your home is worth less to the eventual heirs. This is true unless your home is appreciating in the marketplace in excess of the interest being added monthly to the debt. In this present market it will not be. I truly believe this will be the case for at least a decade or more. Every month your home will be less worth in the market.

Reverse Mortgages interest rates will be around 5%+ yearly, and appreciation will not. And after a few years of falling further and further behind, the appreciation will have to be greater and greater for your equity to simply keep pace and reach break-even.

The "double whammy" is that the market price may be declining monthly as it has in many areas for years, while the debt load is constantly going in the opposite direction. Even if this trend is reversed in five or ten years, the expansion in the market value of the home would have to explode beyond reason to "catch up" with the interest added over time to your debt.

I ALWAYS insist that as many children as possible sit in on the Reverse Mortgage discussions. I have heard of too many couples who have failed to consult their adult children and found the heartache and friction this can cause after the fact. Believe me, it is a REAL consideration, that few ever consider.

Unfortunately there have been many cases of fraud reported in the press where the exact opposite is true. Some kids actually **insist** that their senior parents take out a Reverse Mortgage. Some even suggest it! Then they manage to abscond with the proceeds, by loans or by other sneaky means. I'm not sure which scenario is sadder.

15. HOW TO LOSE YOUR HOME: REPAIRS

Now let's look at the possibility of you losing your home after you get that great-sounding Reverse Mortgage.   How can that possibly happen? Well, there are a number of ways. And believe me, it does happen.

For starters, most senior couples are on a fixed income, often just barely scraping by. The government certainly has not been generous with Social Security increases of late. These older retirees are the ones most likely to consider a Reverse Mortgage.

Property taxes go up every year, sometimes exponentially. While a couple may be able to cover these taxes today, will they be able to do so in ten or twenty years? "No pay taxes, no keep home." Government rule.

Another way to lose your home is to fail to keep up with the maintenance. This is an absolute requirement of the Reverse Mortgage contracts. You are expected to keep the home in exactly the same condition it was in the day you received the mortgage. Can a couple scraping along on a fixed income actually budget for maintenance? Maybe, maybe not. "No maintain home, no keep home". Government rule.

Of course you will be told: "They never check on the maintenance". Try getting **that** in writing!

Speaking of maintenance, this can be a major issue even **before** you get the loan, but **after** you have paid five-hundred bucks or so, non-refundable I might add, for the appraisal. Very often the appraiser will note a number of upgrades and/or repairs that the bank will probably insist upon before making the loan. These can be trivial, or in some cases quite costly. The primary consideration is the safety of the senior occupants. You may believe that your home is 100% fine. The bank, through their appraiser, may not agree.

I know of one case recently where the bank, based upon the appraiser's photographs alone, insisted that two costly staircases be built outside leading to and from a multi-level rose garden. It took a month to complete, and ended up costing the couple $4,581 to comply.

You will never know until **after** the appraisal. If the appraiser thinks you need a new roof, poof, there goes $25,000 up front before you ever see a dime. God forbid there should be some "minor" foundation damage. And if the estimated cost of repairs exceeds 15% of the loan you will be instantly disqualified under another government rule.

Some banks may allow you to sign a "repair addendum" and allow you to do the repairs in a certain amount of time after the loan closes. If you do not, they **will** cancel the loan and take your home.

Sometimes the bank will withhold the repair money from any loan proceeds, and some will even pay the repair contractors directly from these funds. Before you even begin an application process it is a good idea to determine (get it in writing) what the policy on repairs is with the bank in question.

Getting a thorough professional home inspection before applying for a Reverse Mortgage should cost far less than the appraisal and might save you some money, or at least preclude a big surprise.

16.   HOW TO LOSE YOUR HOME: INSURANCE

And what about home insurance? Many couples presently carry minimum insurance or no insurance at all on their homes. It's just too darned expensive. Whoops! Get a Reverse Mortgage and you are immediately compelled to carry **full coverage**. Yipes! Many simply do not budget for this often-considerable added expense. In essence they "self-insure". "No pay insurance, no keep home". Government rule. Many Loan Originators will go out of their way to avoid pointing out this considerable up front expense.

If your home is in a flood zone you will have to carry flood insurance as well. Are you covered for tornados? Earthquakes? You'd better be.

But consider the following:

The government wants the house insured for the full amount of the Reverse Mortgage, which increases steadily. So should your insurance. All the government wants is to be covered in case your house is somehow destroyed. They couldn't care less what happens to you in that unthinkable event.

You might net little or no cash from your Reverse Mortgage depending on paying off any existing forward mortgage, but at least you no longer have mortgage payments. (This might me a lousy trade off relative to your new insurance payments, but that is a different matter.)

The fact is, these are all important considerations, especially when all are added together.

17. HOW TO LOSE YOUR HOME: TAXES

The absolutely fastest way to have a Reverse Mortgage foreclosed is to fail to pay your property taxes on time.

I can tell you from what I have observed on many occasions that if your taxes are due, say, May 1st, and you fail to pay them by May 15th, within two weeks, you will get a threatening letter from the lender.

As in the cases of maintenance and insurance, timely tax payments are mandatory. Government rule. This is why it is imperative that you plan for the future.

Many couples have lost their homes to foreclosure because they could not pay the higher adjusted monthly payment when their forward mortgage "adjusted", after one to five years.   Is a Reverse Mortgage so different?

Your property taxes often adjust upwards every year, even as real appraised values may go down. With States and local municipalities scrambling to find revenue to support social "just causes" and pay for Medicare or whatever, and outrageous public-sector pensions, can you begin to guess where your property taxes will be five or ten years down the road?

Many senior couples are on a fixed income. Cost of Living increases were curtailed in the recent past, and will surely be more so in the future as our economy spirals into even greater crisis. Medical expenses often go up as our age goes up. And property taxes can go up far faster than inflation.

Are you totally convinced that you will be able to pay those increased taxes out of your fixed income? This is something you must consider. Here again, seeking the advice of a qualified professional, be it an elder-care attorney or accountant, or financial planner, makes immense sense.

18.   CAN YOU MANAGE MONEY?

In most cases, any cash received in a Reverse Mortgage will be spent, one way or the other in five or ten years, maybe less. It's called the "Lottery Syndrome".

No matter how many millions are won in the lottery studies show that most winners are broke in a very few years. A Reverse Mortgage can be compared to winning the lottery. But the lottery only costs you a buck a pop. A reverse mortgage can cost you your home

So let's say a few years, or a decade, go by, and you are living with no mortgage payments ever. Fat and happy as a pig in poo. Sounds great, no?

Then, God forbid, you lose your house in a fire or tornado or flood or earthquake. No sweat, right? It's covered by insurance. Well, sort of. The bank and or the government will get the insurance proceeds, not you. Then just try to get financing to rebuild!

You now have no home, no house equity, and no money. You are REALLY up the creek sans paddle. Farfetched?   Not at all. This scenario is even worse if you paid off a forward mortgage and didn't even have the luxury of getting and spending any net proceeds!

When you take out a Reverse Mortgage in today's real estate market you are gambling big time that the market will rebound. (For that matter, so is the lender and the government.) Remember the days not all that long ago when your home was your personal piggy bank? It could be decades, if ever, before we see that scenario again.

As I mentioned earlier, one of the eighty-plus pages of legalese- paperwork in the Reverse Mortgage loan package is a fascinating table that is based on some very optimistic assumptions. If you ever do see this table, study it with a qualified CPA.

See what happens if you plug in some far more conservative estimates of future percentages in market value. Make some realistic assumptions about future property taxes. This one exercise alone will give you great pause in considering a Reverse Mortgage

19.YOUR CREDIT MATTERS

Here is yet another problem with a Reverse Mortgage application. Contrary to what some Loan Originators or ad material will still tell you, that there is "no credit check required", this is no longer strictly true.

Uncle Sap is discovering to their considerable dismay that far too many Reverse Mortgages have been given out to individuals in the past whose fixed incomes simply could not cover the increasing taxes and insurance and maintenance over time. Default and foreclosure was inevitable. Adjustable-mortgage-bubble debacle re-visited!

Foreclosed Reverse Mortgages were not quite what the government expected from this program, in their infinite stupidity. What started the "forward mortgage bubble" in the first place? Individuals whose income could not cover upward-adjusted mortgages. Don't simply blame the banks. Remember, the government mandated that they make those loans.

In fact, when you get a Reverse Mortgage you actually are signing up for TWO separate and distinct mortgages. Surprised? The bank gets one, and the USA gets another. I have never heard that disclosed up front by a salesperson.

One could argue that this just adds to your ward-of-the-state status which includes Social Security, Medicare and any other government benefits you may be receiving. Maybe you don't care.

Personally, I do. The less beholding I am to the State the better I sleep at night.

20.MORTGAGE CANCELLATION?

LOSS BY MANDATE

Could your Reverse Mortgage ever be cancelled against your will? Certainly not by the bank. But what about cancellation by the government? Remember, they also hold a mortgage on your home.

In a National Emergency of some sort, with any President having virtually unlimited power to do anything, are you totally comfortable that a Reverse Mortgage recall could never happen? I'm not.

If you have a nice comfortable big house can you not picture a scenario down the road where the government could MANDATE that other people live in your home because it is "too big" for just the two of you. Far fetched? That precise proposal is under very serious consideration in Great Britain as I write this.

Remember the scene in Dr. Zhivago where the Commissar comes to Yuri's large home with families of "the less fortunate" in tow and introduces Yuri's new mandated tenants? Chilling.?

Incidentally, the actual document package for a Reverse Mortgage is in excess of eighty pages, mostly written in "higher-legalese". I doubt whether one in a hundred Loan Originators have ever taken the time to read every word of these documents, and whether one in ten could answer specific questions relating to the finer points in them.

They are considerably more complex and longer than the extremely-complex forward-mortgage documents! Truly ugly. Few potential Reverse Mortgagees ever read them. Big error. Consult a qualified attorney.

LOSS BY ILL HEALTH

And what about the almost inevitable circumstance in your much later life of being forced by health issues to enter a nursing home or other assisted living facility? "No live in Reverse Mortgaged home, no keep home". Government rule. Definitely worth considering.

21.   THE <u>REAL</u> COST

Ever wonder why a normal "forward" mortgage can be secured, at this writing, for around 3.75%, but you find that a Reverse Mortgage rate can be in the 5%+ range? (Try asking a counselor THAT question!) The fact is that a Reverse Mortgage is VERY, VERY expensive for you, both up front and in the long run through the high interest.

The bank's reasonable rationale for the higher interest rate is the fact that, although the bank is "betting" that you will die according to actuarial-table projection, they are covering their tails in case you just happen to live a very long life beyond statistical expectations. They don't see a dime of profit until everyone on the title is dead.

Even then, if the real estate market never recovers fully, they may make very little money if any. However, they themselves cannot LOSE money, because good old Uncle Sam will take the hit if the equity isn't there to cover the loan balance in full.

Just a thought here that has absolutely nothing to do with this book. Many Reverse

Mortgages were guaranteed by the government at the height of the real estate boom a few years ago. Many of these mortgages are certainly at present "deeply under water" (i.e., a distress sale of the house cannot cover the loan balance) in today's market. This is in spite of the fact that a Reverse Mortgage only initially offered 60% or so of appraised value.

I wonder if this fact is accounted for anywhere in the government's published 16+ trillion dollar debt figure? Perhaps this is part of our $60+ trillion in "other" debt obligations that are sort of swept under the rug. Just wondering.

The "closing costs" for a Reverse Mortgage are not anything like the familiar one thousand dollars or so one has come to expect for a "normal" forward mortgage. Three to ten thousand dollars or more is much closer for the reverse variety, depending upon the price of the house and the greed of the lender. Someone seems to be making out like a bandit. It surely isn't you.

It will be explained to you that your huge up-front costs are due mostly to the fact that you are paying **all** of the mortgage insurance cost up front. "It's not **really** a cost because you get it back pro-rata if you pay off the mortgage early." Really? Fuzzy math. How comforting.

Of course, all of the fees and commissions and insurance are explained away by your Loan Originator as your "opportunity cost". Since it's not out-of-pocket (except for the counseling and appraisal) and because you are "net-**receiving**-money" you are not "really" paying all of these princely sums. That is, at best, more very fuzzy math and warped logic. It may not be out of your pocket now, but it certainly impacts the equity remaining in your home.

Take a long, hard look at these costs, and decide whether you are comfortable with them. You are putting yourself in a position where you cannot protect what should be your most valuable asset in your retirement years.

While you are considering all of the above, see if you can get a straight answer from your Loan Originator/salesperson as to exactly how much money he or she is putting in his or her pocket from your loan transaction.

Not simply "commission", but how much total actual net money, call it what they will. Will he or she put it in writing? If you are dealing directly with a bank's Loan Originator, ask how much bonus he or she is paid for giving you the worst possible deal!

Do you think it is a fair amount for the work performed? Your call. Let me say simply that individuals who focus on Reverse Mortgages today over regular forward mortgages net a lot more money per deal for the minimal extra effort expended.

22.THE LEGAL TITLE TO YOUR HOME

Let's talk about the legal title to your home. This can be a non-issue, or it can be a **really** big issue. For starters, are both spouses on the title? If not, there is probably a VERY good reason for this. It is seldom a simple oversight. I have experienced a number of situations where this was of extreme importance to at least one party.

For example, in the case of a re-married individual who owned the house before a subsequent marriage, putting the "new" spouse on title is often problematic. This may be related to the children of the new spouse, or to some other important issue. Once burned………….

There are two choices: either add the second spouse to the title, OR said second spouse runs the real risk of losing the house when the title holding spouse dies.

In that latter unfortunate event, the surviving spouse has by law just six months to pay off the Reverse Mortgage or sell or refinance the house. That is not a lot of time in this ghastly market. If a number of years have elapsed since the Reverse Mortgage was taken out, the payoff needed may very well be far out of the reach of the surviving not-on-title spouse.

At a senior age, and most likely on a limited fixed income, the possibility of qualifying for a forward mortgage is quite low, even if one has managed to maintain a high credit score.

I have heard from clients that they were told by a bank or Loan Originator in the past: "Oh don't worry, the government won't hold fast to the six-month limit, and would never allow the bank to foreclose under any circumstances". Can you get that in writing? Want to guess? Worth the chance? I think not.

There is one possible reprieve from the above three paragraphs, but it depends on timing and market conditions. Regardless of the outstanding balance on the Reverse Mortgage it may be legally possible for a surviving spouse or heirs to pay only 95% of the then-current appraised market value of the house.

This could be considerably less than the loan balance. I've been told by some banks that this is not true. I am convinced it is the law.

Anyone who finds themselves in this situation in the future should contact HUD (The Department of Housing and Urban Development) and get a final clarification of this point at that particular time. Don't ever take the bank's word for it! Laws change.

Ah, but you say, why not just have the surviving spouse apply for their own Reverse Mortgage? This could possibly work, but is based upon a couple of serious assumptions. For starters, it is rumored that the entire government-guaranteed Reverse Mortgage program could be scrapped in the future, so that option may not even exist if and when one might need it.

It is also rumored that the amount of money available through a Reverse Mortgage at a given age could be reduced from what it is today. So whether a surviving spouse could cover a Reverse Mortgage with a new one is certainly not assured, regardless of age considerations.

Another title issue occurs when there is a wide disparity between the ages of two spouses. I know of many couples whose ages are separated by fifteen to twenty years or more. To qualify for a Reverse Mortgage ALL persons on title must be of the minimum age as prescribed by law, presently 62. The younger spouse MUST come off title if under age 62. Will they be willing to do so? Maybe, maybe not.

I've seen situations where it was no problem at all. I've seen others where there was absolutely no way the younger spouse would consent to dropping off the title to their largest family asset. The risk here to the younger spouse is that in the event of the death of the older spouse the younger spouse must sell or refinance the home as described above.

The age disparity issue even comes up if both spouses are over 62. The amount of money that a reverse Mortgage can bring in is based on the age of the **youngest** qualifying spouse on the title. If, for example, the ages are 82 and 62 or 67 or whatever disparity, the difference in the amount of money available with both spouses on title is much less than if the younger "of-age 62+" spouse is dropped off the title.

One way to obviate this potential problem is for the spouse-on-title to take out a term insurance policy for the amount of the Reverse Mortgage projected out to five or ten years or whatever. This is probably prohibitively expensive, but it is an option.

Here is an interesting scenario I ran across recently. Two senior individuals, each with their own reverse mortgage on their own home, decide to get married (or perhaps just co-habitate). Because a Reverse Mortgage MUST be on a single primary residence, one of those two reverse mortgages must be satisfied before cohabitation. "Satisfied" means either pay off the reverse mortgage in one way or the other, or sell the house.

If the house is "under water", which most are today, the party selling CANNOT owe the bank or government a dime if the house sells for less than the mortgage amount. That is the purpose of the mortgage insurance that was paid for up front. That's the good news. The bad news is that the selling party has given up what in the future might be their only major asset, their home, assuming the real estate market ever actually recovers.

The other bad news is that the "new" spouse who has resolved his or her Reverse Mortgage, cannot be simply **added** to the Reverse Mortgage of the partner with whom they are moving in. Therefore the only consideration is the life or death of the person actually on that Reverse Mortgage. The new spouse is in the position of losing the house upon the death of the Reverse Mortgage holder.

Of course, depending upon the Reverse Mortgage laws of the moment (and they do change, and in fact the program could some day be eliminated entirely) the surviving spouse could get their own Reverse Mortgage to cover the existing one. Or at the time of the marriage they could consider getting an entirely new reverse mortgage with both parties on the title. Costly, but an option.

Let's look at the opposite scenario, a divorce. You think maybe divorces can get rather ugly? Involving a reverse mortgage in the settlement sure doesn't make it any easier! For starters, the reverse mortgage stays in effect until the **last** borrower sells or dies or moves out. Who stays? Who moves? And then we have alimony. Are the proceeds, assuming the reverse mortgage was set up for monthly payments, subject to alimony? Try to get an answer to **that** question from a counselor! Think "Elder Law Attorney".

In fact, I believe that anyone who is even remotely considering a Reverse Mortgage should seek the counsel and guidance of a competent elder-law attorney. Seek an attorney who specializes **only** in elder-law, and ask a few questions to determine how well versed he or she may be on the nuances and possible negatives of Reverse Mortgages. Share this book with them.

Remember, knowledge is power.

23. WILLS AND TRUSTS

A big consideration in choosing a Reverse Mortgage, especially where younger relatives are involved, is **properly** setting up your Wills, or a Revocable LivingTrust and/or Durable Powers of Attorney.

Sadly, most of us eventually go ga-ga. It is in one's best interest to make written provision for someone, usually a son or daughter, to be in charge when you can no longer make decisions in your own best interest.

Just ask any qualified professional, probably best in this case would be elder-care attorney specializing in wills and trusts, whether having a Reverse Mortgage can complicate estate issues. It can, as far as I have been told, but I am far from expert in that area.

Always seek the counsel of qualified professionals.

24. PROBATE

Another consideration that can only be explored with a qualified attorney is the matter of how having a Reverse Mortgage relates to probate after the death of the last surviving title-holder. All of this "legal stuff" can be expensive, but not thoroughly investigating all of it and acting upon the recommendation of qualified counsel, attorney or CPA, can be far more expensive.

Reverse Mortgages may not make sense in the case of very expensive houses. This is because the government sets a limit (presently $625,500) on the amount of proceeds on which your age-related percentage is based. This limit has been changed often in the past and will probably be changed again in the future.

It is very important to note that once you have a Reverse Mortgage it will be virtually impossible to tap what could be considerable additional equity by means of a regular forward second mortgage or an equity line of credit. No lender I can imagine would loan additional funds on a home that is continually losing equity.

When considering a Reverse Mortgage one can choose various combinations of payment. This can range from a line of credit to all-cash, to a lifetime fixed monthly payment, to a larger fixed monthly payment for a set time period to various combinations of all possibilities. Be aware that each option carries with it possible differences in cost, interest rates, and the amount of money you ultimately receive.

There can be significant differences to you which must not be ignored. Do NOT take the word of the Loan Originator/salesperson as to which payment option is "best for you". There is a considerable difference in net commissions to the salesperson between the different options.

You can possibly have the taxes and insurance automatically paid by the bank before you receive any monthly payment. Of course, this last option depletes your equity, if any, even faster.

25. GOVERNMENT BENEFITS

Here is a consideration on which I have had so many different interpretations that I truly have no idea what is true fact. It is possible that there exists no case-law or written government regulations on this matter at all.

The question is: "Does having cash in hand or having an income stream from a Reverse Mortgage have any possible negative effect, a total disqualifier perhaps, on certain means-based government benefits? Can a Reverse Mortgage somehow end up actually **costing** you money or limiting some future benefits?"

This is no small matter, and one that should be discussed with a Certified Public Accountant and perhaps even an attorney prior to innocently and accidentally signing away some valuable present or future benefit. Don't even bother asking any one of the "mandatory government-educated Reverse Mortgage consultants". I have. I could fill up a page with the different answers I have heard!

The same is true for Loan Originators, banks, and mortgage brokers themselves. This is a question that cannot be answered with any degree of certainty, and it could be very critical to your financial future.

The law as I understand it today does not seem to be 100% clear on this issue. But even more important, no one can predict how the law in this regard might change in the future. It is simply a matter of very real concern and importance that is worth factoring in to the Reverse Mortgage "yes/no" equation.

26. IS A REVERSE MORTGAGE EVER OK?

Now let's look at some of the good reasons individuals might actually consider taking out a Reverse Mortgage.

The sports-movie catch-line: "Show Me The Money!" sticks in many minds. If you are considering a Reverse Mortgage because you would like to see some extra cash, and do not have an **urgent** need for that cash, it is a very bad idea for all of the reasons in this report.

In fact, the longer you wait (therefore the older you are) the more money you will be eligible for later on, based upon today's law.

An equally bad reason would be to consider a Reverse Mortgage to pay off a bunch of pesky smaller bills. Try as hard as you can to find other funds to cover these. Trim your budget. Borrow from friends and family. Do whatever you can to avoid risking your home with a Reverse Mortgage.

If you are considering a Reverse Mortgage because you are having trouble paying your existing forward mortgage, I strongly suggest you **very** carefully check all of the government principal-reduction/interest-rate-reduction programs. There are many, and it seems that more are proposed frequently. You may find one that would significantly reduce your monthly payments and make a Reverse Mortgage even less attractive.

Depending upon the State in which you reside (State laws vary greatly), you might even be better off, assuming you can protect your home, to consider some form of bankruptcy protection to obviate your bills. I believe that Texas is one state where you can keep your home in a bankruptcy. There may be others.

Bankruptcy is something you must discuss with a qualified professional, who could be an elder-law attorney, a bankruptcy-specialist attorney, a Certified Public Accountant, financial planner, or some combination thereof.

Incidentally, from my own experience I have found that a bankruptcy per se, even a recent one, is NOT necessarily a disqualifier in obtaining a Reverse Mortgage.

Until you explore ALL of your options, strict budgeting, mortgage modification, and bankruptcy protection, you should not even think for an instant about a Reverse Mortgage.

Always look at a Reverse Mortgage as an **ABSOLUTE LAST RESORT**. Do not make the mistake of listening to the hype that might have you believe that the Reverse Mortgage is a risk-free piggy bank. It's not a cure-all.

27.SCAMS AND IRREGULARITIES

The fees and the interest rates and the amounts of money available from each of the many Reverse Mortgage choices vary greatly. Most lenders offer a variety of programs. Do not allow your Loan Originator (again, read "salesperson") to "suggest" which choice you should make.

You can actually receive a lump sum, a line of credit, or a monthly check of either a fixed amount and term to a lifetime monthly income based upon your age and actuarial tables. In all cases the up-front costs immediately reduce the equity in your home.

The amount of money they earn on your transaction varies **considerably** depending upon which choice "you" decide upon. Want to guess which choice **they** are likely to suggest that you decide upon?

Although it is quite illegal for any licensed person to propose, there are many instances where a senior couple has been encouraged to take out a Reverse Mortgage for no other reason than to have "extra" money to invest (and probably lose) elsewhere, stocks, bonds, annuities or whatever.

A really clever salesperson can make this strategy sound like a no-brainer. So can a sleazy financial planner, in cahoots with an equally sleazy Loan Originator.

In fact it is probably the worst possible advice for any senior citizen. These are the years for caution and conservatism, not the time for risking your home. Run, don't walk, away from such advice.

If the thought of having "investment cash" through a Reverse Mortgage has come to you out of your own mind, please seek the advice of a qualified accountant who will likely refer you to a qualified psychological counselor! I actually had one lady who wanted to get a Reverse Mortgage to have extra money to gamble at the local casino! Truly astonishing.

28. CONCLUSIONS

When would I actually recommend a Reverse Mortgage? First of all, only after someone reads and understands this book! Beyond that, <u>never</u> if you are really desperate for the money. In that case it is always better to sell your home if possible, get as much equity out as possible, and move somewhere more affordable, possibly considering renting.

But if, for example, a foreclosure is imminent, you might "save" your house if you happen to have enough equity in it based on a current appraisal AND you have sufficient income and other assets to comfortably "carry" the taxes and insurance and maintenance <u>well into the future</u>. This is definitely food for a discussion with a good real estate attorney and a Certified Public Accountant before you proceed or sign anything relating to a Reverse Mortgage.

What if you do have sufficient future income and assets, AND lots of home equity AND no mortgage to consider? You fully understand the possible downsides shared in this book. Well, this is a nice position to be in! **IF**, and only if, this is your situation, I can think of a few rationales for actually taking out a Reverse Mortgage.

First rationale is if you need the money for absolutely necessary very-expensive medical expenses for yourself, a spouse or a family member not covered by any insurance plan. A truly life or death situation. In this case a Reverse Mortgage could be literally a life-saver.

In a lighter vein, if you have lots of assets and are comfortable in your ability to "carry" the Reverse Mortgage and couldn't care less about the possible negatives expressed above, and want to take a long world-wide vacation, or use the money to complete your "bucket list" and don't want to tap into you're your existing assets to pay for it, then I say GO FOR IT!

Reverse Mortgages have actually been around for a half-century. For the most part over much of this time these were private-money Reverse Mortgages, though some banks participated. It was not until the presidency of Bush the Younger that the Federal Government stepped in to guarantee these loans. Today around 100,000 Reverse

Mortgages are done yearly by the banks, with none that I know of being done privately.

Initially conceived for older seniors, until recently most Reverse Mortgages were assumed by seniors in their 70s. In this present awful economy, there has been a huge shift to the earliest possible 60s. Even some financial planners are steering their young-senior clients in this direction. Very, very bad advice.

Big mistake. In twenty years or more, a very realistic life expectancy today, these now-older-seniors will have absolutely nothing left of what is normally their greatest asset....their home. Not a good scenario in which to spend your most golden years.

One last point. It true you can never owe more than the house sells for. But is it fair for people with forward mortgages to have their mortgages modified by reducing the principal owed? Then, when they sell their home in the future, they could get more money than they would have had the principal not been reduced.

But what about Reverse Mortgages?   If they reduced the principal of your Reverse Mortgage you might then be in the position of not only covering the loan, but actually walking away with some cash. Why should that be any different from a forward mortgage? From what I have been told it will simply never happen.

You are stuck for life with a mortgage that **increases** every month and will never be modified downward. This steadily **decreases** the chance of you ever seeing any equity in the future should you decide to sell.

Here's a "what if" question that I have never had answered to my satisfaction. What happens to your Reverse Mortgage if the bank holding the note goes under? Bank of America has done thousands of these (they stopped in 2011) and is a bank that is reported to be in serious financial trouble, so the scenario itself is not far-fetched. But assuming Uncle Sam steps in as now the only note holder of record are there any implications?

Of course there is always the very real possibility that the United States itself could go out of business, that is, default on everything and sell off assets. With its unimaginable 16+

trillion dollar debt and 60+ trillion in unfunded obligations many consider this inevitable. What happens to your Reverse Mortgage then? Or to your home?

Does the government hold a fire-sale of every property to which they can lay claim? Scary, but I'd prefer they not hold any note over my head ever.

Think of a Reverse Mortgage as winning a lottery. BUT instead of simply being right back to square one after you piss away your winnings as most will do, you now unnecessarily have put the very roof over your head at serious risk. What is the probably biggest reason to NOT consider a Reverse Mortgage?

It is called "human nature". A big problem that rears its ugly head with many lottery winners is the fact that most find some way to spend it all and end up right back where they started. Persons unaccustomed to managing large sums of money are almost certain to find creative ways to lose it all.

So there you have it. Knowing the dangers, the pros and cons, drawbacks, downside and disadvantages, it is your choice. Think as hard and long about this choice as you have ever pondered any financial decision in your lifetime. It is your most important decision of all.

And remember, even AFTER closing escrow on a Reverse Mortgage Loan you have THREE DAYS, called your "right of rescission" period, to change your mind and cancel the entire matter without any penalty. Of course you'll be out whatever you spent on counseling, appraisal, and mandatory upgrades, but cancelling may be the best decision you ever made!

PLEASE THINK TWICE BEFORE MAKING A MISTAKE YOU MAY WELL LIVE TO REGRET. REVERSE MORTGAGES MAKE REAL SENSE FOR ONLY A VERY FEW INDIVIDUALS. YOU ARE PROBABLY NOT ONE OF THEM. DON'T PUT YOUR FUTURE AT RISK. "JUST SAY NO!"

ABOUT THE AUTHOR

Jim Anderson has been a Loan Originator for over fifteen years, and has specialized in Reverse Mortgages. It's in his genes. His father worked for the same mortgage processor for over fifty years! For the past four years Jim has been mortgage licensed in Arizona, after five years as a Loan Officer in Hawaii. He focuses exclusively on Reverse Mortgages.

In addition, Jim has been directly involved in real estate as a builder/developer, Broker, and trainer for over forty years. He was the Education Committee Chairman for the Kona Hawaii Board of Realtors where he taught the many nuances of Reverse Mortgages.

As Broker In Charge (BIC) of the largest real estate company on the Big Island he trained salespersons in Reverse Mortgage methodology. He is a graduate of the Real Estate Institute (GRI), and presently runs his own local real estate company, mortgage company, and insurance brokerage.

Born in Brooklyn, New York's Bedford Stuyvesant ghetto, he graduated from The Polytechnic Institute (now NYU-Poly) with an engineering degree. He went on to earn his Master's Degree at CCNY. Both degrees were earned in night school while working full-time days to support his family!

After a successful thirty- year career, mostly in upper-level Fortune 500 management, Jim decided to leave the "rat race" and start his own businesses. A published author since 1970, he has written eleven books and countless articles. He has been published in *Leaders* magazine, which is sent only to heads of state and corporate CEOs.

An often-awarded photographer, he is an accomplished SCUBA diver and private pilot, and champion amateur golfer. He is proud of his past service with the Civil Air Patrol. His hobbies include astronomy and rock-hounding.

With a strong belief in "giving back", Jim has served on the Boards of Directors of many local non-profit groups. He is a proud member of American Legion Post #66, having served in the Army during the Vietnam era. He is one of the original members of MENSA.

Married to his beautiful wife Melanie for thirty years, he has four children and two lovely grandchildren. Jim and Mel live on a remote ranch in the high Sonoran Desert with their two great pups.

In his 75th year and very comfortably "retired", his pet peeve is the fact that seniors are so often taken advantage of financially. He believes that Reverse Mortgages fall into the category of financial products that are sold to seniors as the "best thing ever", and are in fact anything but that.

He hopes **Reverse Mortgage Dangers** will offer some helpful guidance for seniors in the process of making this important decision.

We wish him well!

CPSIA information can be obtained at www.ICGtesting.com
Printed in the USA
LVOW101453180413

329845LV00020B/1179/P